DRAW IN NEARER

An Adult Coloring Bible Study

Written by Leslie Eaton

Illustrations and Artwork by Nicole Plymesser Nelson

Bible Stories from the Heart™
Suwanee, GA

DRAW IN NEARER

Bible Stories from the Heart
1232 Fieldcrest Court
Suwanee, GA 30024

www.biblestoriesfromtheheart.com

Printed in the United States of America

ISBN 0998090557

Contents

Introduction

Bible Stories from the Heart incorporates reading, writing, and artwork to help you meditate and pray over God's scripture in a deep and meaningful way.

There is a reason we spend several days over the same scripture. Our Bible study is written as a way to deepen your comprehension and enhance your daily quiet time with God. It is our goal for you to savor God's word, not rush through it. We want each of you to take the time to FEEL God's love.

The study is designed to complete either with a small group or as an independent study. As an independent study, you are free to work at your own pace.

You may complete the study in a few days, a few weeks, or maybe months. ALL ARE GOOD. The important thing is to go deeper with GOD and let HIM fill your heart.

Feel free to invite a few friends to join you, or complete this study alone. Either way, get prepared for some amazing God moments through this amazing Bible study!

We would love for you to participate in our Bible Stories from the Heart group on Facebook. There, you can share your artwork, fellowship with others doing our studies and participate in our regular online studies as well. You'll be connected with a dynamic, supportive and highly engaged community of over 8,000 women. Just enter **Bible Stories from the Heart** in the Facebook search bar and you'll find us!

If you would like to purchase additional pdf files of our studies for small group use, they can be found at www.biblestoriesfromtheheart.com.

Important: if you would like to be notified of future publications and receive regular devotions, please sign up for our free email club! www.biblestoriesfromtheheart.com.

Thank you for joining us!

Meet the Writers

LESLIE EATON - Leslie will lead you through the reading and study of each lesson. She has over 20 years of experience as a professional educator. Ten of those years she served as a reading comprehension specialist. Leslie has undergone extensive training in both reading comprehension and effective learning strategies. She is now excited to bring these successful strategies to this study. Her goal is to empower people as they seek to experience God's love on a deeper level. She has led various Christian small groups and book studies in and around the Atlanta area for over 5 years. Now she is bringing her knowledge of teaching and her love of God's Word to Bible Stories from the Heart.

What to expect from Leslie:

You will be lead through each scripture lesson with one goal in mind - to know and understand God's love for you!

What we will do:

- Read Scriptures that are listed
- Reflect on the key verses contained in each lesson
- Answer discussion questions found with each lesson

What we will learn:

- Meaning of key words
- Relevant Biblical history
- Connection to our lives today

 NICOLE PLYMESSER NELSON - Nicole has been teaching art for 20 years—in elementary and high schools, retail settings, private lessons, and workshops. All along she has written her own curriculum that works for all ages and abilities. Nicole also has a successful illustration business that showcases her faith. She designs the illustrations for the studies so that all audiences will feel comfortable using art to study God's Word.

What to expect from Nicole:

The goal is for you to use art methods to meditate, pray and connect with God on an even deeper level - taking time to create will allow God to flow through your hands and fingers as you ALLOW HIS WORDS to INSPIRE YOU! As you work, pray over the images and words. Brain science shows that creating artwork actually creates more connections in the brain, making information easier to remember. You will be amazed at how this transforms your study and recall of the lessons!

Three options are available for you:

- Read the scriptures and create your own design in your Bible or journal.
- Use the coloring page versions - adding color in your media of choice.
- Or use the mini versions to trace into your Bible or faith art journal.

Why Our Studies Work

The Bible is a Book of LOVE.

If we are not careful, we may neglect to see God's Love in the scriptures that we read.

At Bible Stories from the Heart we never want this to happen. It is our goal to view every word found in the Bible as a piece of a love letter written especially for us. Because of this, we are very intentional in the way that we write and pace our lessons and art activities.

The devotions we will be studying will move us very slowly through certain passages of the Bible. In each lesson we will spend time reading and reflecting upon key words found in our focus verses. Doing this will help you to actually relate God's Word to your life and will help you to feel His love on a much deeper level.

We believe that the BEST way to study God's Word and REALLY absorb it is to take the time to reflect upon it and then allow it to flow THROUGH you as you read!!

LOVE is a verb - it is ACTION... it is not STAGNANT!!!

Consider for a minute the difference between the Dead Sea and the Sea of Galilee. Life does not exist in the Dead Sea, yet The Sea of Galilee THRIVES. What is the major difference between these two bodies of water? The Dead Sea has NO outlet and no action!

We must remember this fact and apply it whenever we spend time with the Lord.

One way to allow God's LOVE to flow through you as you study the Bible is to DOODLE or COLOR as you read.

There is something very powerful about reflecting and creating while reading.

Our Strategy: Reflective Bible Study

Each week we will focus on a different scripture. You will read and re-read that scripture several times over the week.

The purpose behind re-reading scripture is for you to intentionally spend time reflecting and meditating on God's deep and powerful love for you.

We believe that we should **meditate on the Word of God DAILY.**

We believe that the Word of God should be *savored* not gulped.

We know that the concepts in each verse are given to us from the Holy Spirit! They are meant to *guide us* and *change us.*

It is up to us to actually allow that to happen.

In order to read God's Word as intended, we must intentionally *MEDITATE* on its concepts.

David learned this in his life as did Joshua:

Psalms 119:15-16 (NKJV)
I will meditate on Your precepts and regard Your ways. I shall delight in Your statutes; I shall not forget Your word.

Joshua 1:8 (NKJV)
This Book of the Law shall not depart from your mouth, but you shall meditate in it day and night, that you may observe to do according to all that is written in it.

Our Goal

Our goal is to help you establish a deep and loving relationship with our Savior. Relationships are intentional! The best relationships develop slowly over time.

As we continue in this study, we do not want to rush through the lessons. Let's intentionally take our time and enjoy every moment that we spend in the presence of the Lord! Let's remember that <u>we are building a relationship, not earning a grade</u>. So, let's just relax and enjoy the journey!

How can we build a deeper relationship with Christ?

<u>Consider this:</u>

When you first meet a new friend or co-worker do you automatically trust this person?

Of course not! Trust is something that is built and grows over time.

The more time you spend with a person, the more time trust has to grow. As you spend time together, this new person will have various opportunities to display their loyalty, honesty, and abilities to you.

If enough of these qualities are displayed, trust begins to grow. Then every time you notice these qualities displayed again, trust grows deeper.

It is the same with God. Authentic trust is built over time. To build this trust, we must take the time to observe and discover the true character of God.

We can accomplish this by using two simple strategies:

1. Intentional Bible Study (searching for God's love)

2. Reflective Journal Writing (reflecting on God's love / S.O.A.P.)

Our Love-Directed Approach

Intentional Bible Study

Bible study which intently looks for the character traits of God is vital.

God is LOVE! God never changes! He is and will ALWAYS be LOVE!

So, what exactly is love?

1 Corinthians 13:4-8 (NKJV)
4 Love suffers long and is kind; love does not envy; love does not parade itself, is not puffed up; 5 does not behave rudely, does not seek its own, is not provoked, thinks no evil; 6 does not rejoice in iniquity, but rejoices in the truth; 7 bears all things, believes all things, hopes all things, endures all things. 8 Love never fails…

LOVE-Directed Bible Study Strategy

Read each verse of the Bible with a specific purpose - To see LOVE!

If we focus on this, we will see that EVERYTHING God has ever done or will EVER do; he does out of his intense LOVE for his children.

Wherever there is LOVE - there is God!

S.O.A.P. (Scripture, Observation, Application, Prayer)

Reflective Journal Writing

S.O.A.P. is an acronym which stands for Scripture, Observation, Application and Prayer. This technique is a powerful way to reflect on and absorb more of the verses from each lesson that speak to you.

There is a SOAP reflection page near the end of each lesson which you may use to write down your own thoughts. We've included an example below to better illustrate how the SOAP pages might be used.

The following scripture in this example is not in this study. It has been chosen for demonstration purposes.

<u>SOAP Reflection (Scripture)</u>

(S) Scripture:

Exodus 14:13-14 (NKJV)
13 And Moses said to the people, "Do not be afraid. Stand still, and see the salvation of the Lord, which He will accomplish for you today. For the Egyptians whom you see today, you shall see again no more forever. 14 The Lord will fight for you, and you shall hold your peace."

<u>SOAP Reflection (Observation)</u>

(O) Observation:

As a result of bad choices made by the Israelites, they were taken as slaves in Egypt for several years. After receiving word from God to do so, the Israelites are attempting to escape from their Egyptian captives. The Israelites are scared. They know that if they are caught they will be tortured or even killed for their rebellion.

I observe GOD'S LOVE in this verse! Moses is telling the Israelites to not be afraid, to stand firm, and that God will deliver them from their enemies. God is willing and able to lead them to safety - this is LOVE!

This verse PROVES that God was willing and able to rescue his children from hardships. Since God NEVER changes, he is still able and willing to rescue me! This strong anchor will help me stand firm when any future strong winds blow.

SOAP Reflection (Application)

(A) Application:

Just like the Israelites I made some bad choices in the past which led me into captivity. Unlike the Israelites, my captivity was more mental than physical. My mental captivity was a result of a past affair and other bad choices which surrounded that affair. As a result of these bad choices, Satan was able to temporarily bind me! During and even after the fallout from my affair, the devil worked to convince me that I was an evil person who was unworthy of love.

Even though I knew that God had forgiven me, Satan tried to keep me captive to my past. For a while I felt trapped in self - loathing! Eventually through my pain I reached out to God. I began reading and studying the Word of God like I never had before.

I had read the Bible in the past, but this time was different. This time when I read scripture I was actually reading for a purpose. My goal was to see if I was indeed unlovable! What God revealed to me was the EXACT opposite! God LOVED me more than I could ever even begin to understand. Through the blood of Christ, my past sin would not keep me shut off from his love!

This was so beautiful to me! God used water to rescue the Israelites and he used BLOOD to rescue me! I began to feel lovable again. I found that the more time I spent in God's Word the less I felt trapped in my past.

Eventually I felt totally free! God RELEASED me!

All my Lord needed was for me to grow DEEP roots in his LOVE. Then he did the rest. Now God's LOVE is able to both FILL me and FLOW through me! I now know that I am indeed LOVED!

I am now able to both receive true love and to give love.

This is because God has filled me with HIS LOVE!

I now know that nothing I will do will make my Heavenly Father love me any less!

I feel so FREE! I am no longer a CAPTIVE!

SOAP Reflection (Prayer)

(P) Prayer:

Dear Lord, thank you for loving me. Thank you for forgiving me of my past sin and setting me free! Please help me to continue to grow my spiritual roots deeper and deeper into your love. Please be with me during this study. Speak to me in bold new ways. Help me to hear and respond in positive ways to your loving voice. In Jesus name I pray, Amen.

Our God ADORES each one of us! Our God is LOVE! Take a few minutes now to write your own SOAP reflection journal entry on this same verse. As we continue in this study, let's focus our hearts and minds on GOD'S AMAZING LOVE!

We encourage you to use these "LOVE-DIRECTED" Bible study strategies throughout this study (and beyond).

Reflection Questions:

1. What am I hoping to get from this Bible Study?

2. Do I feel like I have an actual relationship with Christ? Why or why not?

3. What have I done in the past to try to build a closer relationship with God?

4. Am I willing to try a new approach to Bible Study?

Small Group Suggestions

To use this study in a small group setting we recommend the following:

1. As a group, meet one day per week.
2. Provide time for hospitality then open the group in prayer.
3. Each meeting will follow a set schedule:

Lesson Time:
- Introduce the lesson and have everyone open their workbooks. Give members about 10 minutes to read the lesson. Encourage everyone to jot down their thoughts directly on the lesson pages as they go.
- After the lesson is read, allow time for members to share their thoughts with the group.
- Then read a few discussion questions to the group and give time to discuss and provide collaborative feedback. Encourage everyone to participate.

Art Time:
- Allow time to get out all art supplies and preview the weekly art example. Members can choose to bring any art materials that they wish: watercolors, crayons, colored pencils, markers, etc. There is no one way to create the weekly art pieces.
- Members are encouraged to create their art in their own Faith Journal. Keeping the art pieces together is a wonderful way to document their spiritual growth and will make it easier for them to continue this process after this study ends.
- Play soft music in the background and allow members time to reflect on God's Word as they create their own art. You may recreate Nicole's piece exactly, or create any other picture that flows from them. If anyone is leery about their creativity, they may simply color one of the coloring sheets which are provided for each lesson.

Meeting Conclusion:
- The meeting will end with members sharing their art and thoughts with the group.
- Each member will leave the meeting with an understanding of how to use their SOAP reflection page. They will be encouraged to go deeper into God's Word in the next few days by reading the given scripture and then reflecting upon it.

As each week passes, it will become easier and more natural for members of the group to both reflect on, and interact with the Word of God.

Example Schedule

Hours of the day can be adjusted to fit your schedule.

7:00-7:30   Snacks and social time

7:35-7:40   Open in prayer and welcome members

7:40-7:50   Encourage members to interact with the text they are about to read by underlining important words and actually writing their thoughts and questions on the lesson page as they read.

7:50-8:00   Members read the weekly lesson

8:00-8:10   Read a few of the questions and allow discussion

8:10-8:15   Get out art supplies and preview weekly art piece

8:15-9:00   Play soft music and allow time for members to meditate, pray, and create their art

9:00-9:15   Share art pieces and thoughts

9:15-9:30   Pass out SOAP pages and close in prayer

Hospitality Ideas

1. Serve a light snack each week. Members can volunteer to bring finger foods or desserts on a rotating basis, if desired.

2. Offer a variety of both sugary and non-sugary drinks.

3. Have plenty of plastic cups, paper plates, as well as napkins.

4. Have name tags ready for members to fill out and wear.

5. Remember people are coming for a purpose: to connect with others and to connect with God. Be sure that all members are introduced and feel welcome.

6. Have chairs set in a circle formation to promote easy conversation throughout the lesson.

7. Provide an "ice breaker" activity for the first few meetings: there are several fun ideas found on Google (Christian small group ice breaker activities).

8. Make sure you have an area designated for the art activity. You may need to provide paper towels and plastic cups of water for watercolor paints (if needed).

9. Have a few extra boxes of crayons or colored pencils on hand in case members forget their art supplies.

Suggested Art Supplies

These are a few of Nicole's favorites but you can use any materials of your choice.

Paper: ANY kind of paper will work! Even just a basic notebook or typing paper, some may decide to do the art directly in a journaling Bible. But a separate sketchbook has several positives: you will have a book of all of your favorite verses, you can do them over and over, plus you will have space to add extra journaling as well. Canson mixed media brand is my all-time favorite due to the bright whiteness of this paper and it holds up to watercolors well.

Paints and brushes: any brand works, travel or school sets, or use the tubes of watercolor in a palette (squirt them into the pans and let them dry before use). You will want three brushes for sure: a one inch flat, a round brush, and a pointed brush.

Collage paper: Use old dictionaries from thrift stores, receipts, homework from kids, anything! Mod Podge or good old Scotch craft glue work best. Glue sticks work, but can release with watercolor on top.

Writing Utensils: There are a few different options.

- **Pen Options: Pilot G-2** in 10 for nice, black, even flow gel pen to journal and write prayers. **Sakura Black Glaze pens** or **Sharpie fine pen/markers** for outlining and large words.

- **Magic Rub Eraser** from Prismacolor.

- **Colored Pencils:** Prismacolor (artist grade) or Crayola (student grade) are your best bets depending on your budget.

Additional Resources

We have provided a number of additional online resources for your use.

PDF Copies of Workbooks - come in handy for those who wish to print multiple copies of the coloring pages, SOAP pages, etc. If you would like additional pdf copies of this workbook, they are available at www.biblestoriesfromtheheart.com.

Email Club - By signing up for our email club, you will receive weekly devotions, inspirational messages, art activities, exclusive offers and advance notification of new studies.

Facebook Group – if you haven't already done so, we hope you will join us on Facebook! Just type Bible Stories from the Heart into the Facebook search bar and you'll find us! You'll be connected with an engaged group of women who participate in our studies. We would love for you to post your artwork to share with the rest of the group!

Video Interview - You can learn more about our ministry by watching this video which is on the Bible Stories from the Heart YouTube page.

Bible Stories from the Heart atlantalive2016interview
Bible Stories from the Heart
2 months ago · 1,788 views
Interview on Atlanta Live explaining our faith art Bible Studies for adults

Website – where you will find more information on our Facebook group, art tutorials, coloring pages and more: **www.biblestoriesfromtheheart.com**

Art Examples

Week One Lesson

Week One Introduction

Does God even like spending time with his children?

For some of us, this is a question that may stop us from drawing closer to our Heavenly Father.

The remarkable fact is that God truly does want to spend every minute with us. There is never a moment in time when our Heavenly Father would rather be doing anything else other than being in fellowship with us. He is deeply in love with each one of us- we are his beloved children!

Let's look closely at both Jesus' words and actions in this week's lesson to help us to see this more clearly.

Focus Scriptures

Luke 10:38-42 (NKJV)

<u>Mary and Martha</u>

38 Now it happened as they went that He entered a certain village; and a certain woman named Martha welcomed Him into her house. 39 And she had a sister called Mary, who also sat at Jesus' feet and heard His word. 40 But Martha was distracted with much serving, and she approached Him and said, "Lord, do You not care that my sister has left me to serve alone? Therefore, tell her to help me."

41 And Jesus answered and said to her, "Martha, Martha, you are worried and troubled about many things. 42 But one thing is needed, and Mary has chosen that good part, which will not be taken away from her."

Biblical History

Jesus and his disciples often traveled. As they traveled, they would often stay at the homes of fellow believers. During each visit, Jesus would fellowship with the families He stayed with.

Jesus had stayed with Mary and Martha on other travels before. He cared for their family very much. Earlier in His ministry Jesus had actually raised their brother Lazarus from the dead.

Mary and Martha both loved Jesus very deeply.

<u>Meaning behind their names:</u>

Martha means 'lady of the house'

Mary means 'wise woman' or 'lady'; it is a Greek form of the Hebrew Miriam or Mariam.

You may find it is interesting that the sister with the "wise" name was the one who showed true wisdom in this situation when she chose to sit at the feet of Jesus.

Thoughts from Leslie

It is important to note that God deeply desires for each one of us to draw nearer to Him. We saw this as we read the story of Mary and Martha. Our Heavenly Father truly does LOVE us. He sincerely wants to be close to us.

This may seem like a small detail at first, but it is not. This is a HUGE and VITAL realization! Think about it, why would any of us choose to move closer to someone that does not care about us?

I don't know about you, but I never want to intentionally move closer to someone if they do not want me near to them. I never want to feel like I am a burden or imposition on anyone. Knowing that my Lord and Savior truly does want me near to Him helps me be both willing and eager to spiritually move closer to Him.

Let's reflect upon the story of Mary and Martha.

Reflection Number One

God WANTS us near to Him.

Jesus has come to the home of Mary and Martha.

What is His purpose in being there? Let's look closely to find the answer.

Jesus and His disciples are traveling. They do not own houses in the different towns in which they travel, so they choose to stay with other believers.

It is important to note that Jesus did not NEED to stay with anyone as He travels. He is the Son of God! He actually created the entire world and everything in it simply by speaking it into existence.

Reflecting on this fact helps us to realize that Jesus could have chosen to simply speak the words and He could have provided food and shelter for Himself and His companions at any time without needing to stay with anyone.

Not long before arriving at the home of Mary and Martha, Jesus had fed 5,000 people with only five loaves of bread and two fish. This should prove to us that He definitely had the ability to personally provide everything that He and His disciples would ever need during their travels in the same exact way.

It is imperative that we understand that Jesus chose to abide with others not because He NEEDED to, but because He WANTED to. He invites us to abide with Him today for the same reason.

This should help us realize that Jesus truly does DESIRE to STAY CLOSE to us.

Reflection Number Two

We do not need to "earn our spot" before we draw nearer to God.

Jesus wants for us to *stay close* to Him not because He needs our hands, but simply because He desires our heart.

It is important for us to realize that there is nothing that we can do to earn our spot near Jesus. This realization is sometimes difficult for us to believe. In this crazy world, we begin to believe that LOVE is something we must earn. This warped thinking tricks us into believing that the one who works the hardest for Jesus is the one who will be chosen to abide in His presence.

It is this thinking that makes most of us relate to Martha in this story. As we read these verses many of us find ourselves feeling sorry for hard working Martha and maybe even a little angry at her sister Mary.

Isn't it sad that as women we tend to believe that acts earn love? Women, as a whole, grow up thinking that that the best way to make someone love them is by serving them more and more.

Serving others is definitely important. The problem comes when we try to base and grow a relationship simply through works. Relationships are built through quality time spent with another. Doing things for people should never replace quality time spent with them. This is the big takeaway from the story of Mary and Martha.

Serving will never move us closer to someone, it will only make us feel more needed. God doesn't need any of us. He desires for each of us to abide with Him, because He loves us not because He needs us! Because of this, drawing closer to Jesus can only be accomplished by becoming less like Martha and more like Mary.

As we continue in this study let's focus our attention on reflecting upon the beliefs and actions of Mary. Like Mary, we must first believe that Jesus truly does desire to be near to us. She believed that Jesus wanted to spend time with her so she intentionally chose to move closer to Him.

Next, let's take note that Mary did not try to earn her spot at the feet of Jesus. We must realize the same. To truly be near to Jesus, we must focus less on work and more on fellowship. It is important that each of us truly understand that it is God's LOVE which calls and allows us to come to Him. We do not earn our new spot by the work of our hands!

Our God longs to have a personal relationship with each one of us just as He did so many years ago with Mary and Martha. He is reaching out for us to come closer. Isn't this AMAZING?

Focus Words

We will focus on one word Monday through Thursday in order to gain a greater understanding of each verse. On Friday, will devote time to reflecting on the previous week and doing the SOAP activity.

MONDAY

Luke 10:38-42 (NKJV)

Mary and Martha

38 Now it happened as they went that He entered a certain village; and a certain woman named Martha **welcomed** *Him into her house. 39 And she had a sister called Mary, who also sat at Jesus' feet and heard His word. 40 But Martha was distracted with much serving, and she approached Him and said, "Lord, do You not care that my sister has left me to serve alone? Therefore, tell her to help me."*

41 And Jesus answered and said to her, "Martha, Martha, you are worried and troubled about many things. 42 But one thing is needed, and Mary has chosen that good part, which will not be taken away from her."

Welcomed: (verb)
to receive or accept with pleasure; regard as pleasant or good

Original Word: δέχομαι (hupodechomai)

Definition: I take, receive, accept, welcome.

Connection to Us

Martha "welcomed" Jesus into her home. She did this by physically inviting Jesus in. Many of us today also "welcome" Jesus into our home. We do this by purchasing Bibles, devotion books, prayer journals, and the like. Like Martha, we truly desire to spend time with Jesus. And like Martha, we easily become distracted. With every new day, our Savior is calling for us to move nearer to Him.

We can do this by spending time with Him reading His Holy Word and meditating on His love. Will we move nearer to our Savior today? Will we momentarily leave our distractions behind to accomplish this goal? Jesus is waiting with open arms. The next step is up to us!

I'd like to encourage you to write down any thoughts you have on how this connects to you. Making notes like this will be a helpful reference for you in your future.

Connection to Me

_____

_____

_____

_____

_____

_____

TUESDAY

Luke 10:38-42 (NKJV)

Mary and Martha

38 Now it happened as they went that He entered a certain village; and a certain woman named Martha welcomed Him into her house. 39 And she had a sister called Mary, who also sat at Jesus' feet and **heard** His word. 40 But Martha was distracted with much serving, and she approached Him and said, "Lord, do You not care that my sister has left me to serve alone? Therefore, tell her to help me."

41 And Jesus answered and said to her, "Martha, Martha, you are worried and troubled about many things. 42 But one thing is needed, and Mary has chosen that good part, which will not be taken away from her."

Heard: (verb)
to learn by the ear or by being told; be informed of.

Original word: ἀκούω (akouō)

Definition: to hear (in various senses)

Connection to Us

Mary did not just listen to Jesus speak, she HEARD His words. This is vital for us to understand. Hearing involves learning! Mary learned from Jesus. This should be our goal today.

Let's strive to intentionally be like Mary each and every day. Let's open our ears and hearts and allow Jesus to teach us!

We can do this as we actively read God's Word and reflect upon it.

By READING God's truths and then REFLECTING and APPLYING them, we can be like Mary in our daily relationship with Christ!

Are we ready to LEARN from our Savior? Are we ready to be filled with the LOVE of Jesus?

Let's spend some quiet time reading and meditating on God's Word today!

Connection to Me

_____

_____

_____

_____

_____

_____

WEDNESDAY

Luke 10:38-42 (NKJV)

Mary and Martha

38 Now it happened as they went that He entered a certain village; and a certain woman named Martha welcomed Him into her house. 39 And she had a sister called Mary, who also sat at Jesus' feet and heard His word. 40 But Martha was **distracted** with much serving, and she approached Him and said, "Lord, do You not care that my sister has left me to serve alone? Therefore, tell her to help me."

41 And Jesus answered and said to her, "Martha, Martha, you are worried and troubled about many things. 42 But one thing is needed, and Mary has chosen that good part, which will not be taken away from her."

Distracted: (adjective)
to be drawn away or diverted, as the mind or attention.

Original word: περισπάω (perispaō)

Definition: to drag all around, i.e. (figuratively) to distract (with care)

Connection to Us

As women, we consider ourselves to be "masters" of multi-tasking. The truth is, when we use this mindset in our relationships, we are actually "masters" of none.

When we focus our attention on more than one thing at a time, nothing or no one is getting our FULL attention. In our busy lives this is often necessary, but can be harmful in our relationships. Relationships are about giving yourself completely to another person. We cannot give ourselves completely to another person if our minds are diverted during "quality" time spent with them. Mary knew the importance of devoting a few minutes out of her day completely focused on Jesus. It is vital that each day we find time to do the same. Our Savior desires a DEEP relationship with us. He wants us to come to him each day (even for as little as a 15- minute time period.)

Are we ready to schedule 15 minutes of time each day completely in the presence of LOVE? Let's take a few minutes now to quietly meditate on the truths found in this week's scripture.

Connection to Me

_____

_____

_____

_____

_____

_____

THURSDAY

*38 Now it happened as they went that He entered a certain village; and a certain woman named Martha welcomed Him into her house. 39 And she had a sister called Mary, who also sat at Jesus' feet and heard His word. 40 But Martha was distracted with much **serving**, and she approached Him and said, "Lord, do You not care that my sister has left me to serve alone? Therefore, tell her to help me."*

41 And Jesus answered and said to her, "Martha, Martha, you are worried and troubled about many things. 42 But one thing is needed, and Mary has chosen that good part, which will not be taken away from her."

Serving: (verb)
furnishing or supplying with something needed or desired

Original Word: διακονέω (diakonia)

Definition: to be an attendant, i.e. wait upon (menially as a host, or friend)

Connection to Us

As women we tend to show love by serving or "providing".

We begin this habit from an early age. As children we show love to our parents and friends by "making" them things: crafts, notes, desserts, and doing things for them. We continue these habits as adults. The more we LOVE someone, the more we tend to want to DO for them. Sometimes we even judge how much someone else loves us by calculating how much they "do" for us. This is not how Jesus determines LOVE!

Jesus does not NEED us to provide for Him to prove our love for Him. What Jesus most desires is US! He simply wants us to spend time each day in HIS presence!!!

This is so AMAZING! Jesus simply desires us to be NEAR! Are you ready to draw nearer to Him today?

Connection to Me

_____

_____

_____

_____

_____

_____

Strategy for This Week: Drawing Nearer

Drawing nearer to our Heavenly Father is the ultimate goal of this study.

We learned through the story of Mary and Martha that God truly does want us near to him. Now that we know He desires us to come closer, let's consider what is needed to actually accomplish this.

We see through the actions of Mary that quiet fellowship with our Lord is what is needed on an ongoing basis to help us to move closer. For this reason, our strategy for this entire study is *fellowship*

But before we can fellowship, we need to clear our minds. To help us to do this, we can color. There have been many studies completed recently which prove that coloring can actually help to quiet a person's thoughts.

Knowing this, Bible Stories from the Heart provides a coloring page at the end of every lesson.

Feel free to color the picture provided, or simply quiet your mind and doodle.

Are you ready to begin? Grab some crayons let's get started!!

As you color:

- Allow yourself to fellowship with Jesus.
- As you create your beautiful art, focus your thoughts on God's love for you.
- Allow yourself to move closer to His loving presence.
- Listen quietly as He reveals new truths to you.
- Thank Him for his burning LOVE for you!

Come Unto Me
By Deborah Ann Belka

Come unto Me, my child . . .
such sweet music to my ears
Come unto Me, Jesus calls . . .
O' how these words, I love to hear.

Come unto Me, my daughter . . .
such tenderness, Jesus has for me
Come unto Me, His words are like . . .
sweet nectar to a honeybee.

Come unto Me, my beloved . . .
such comfort in three little words
Come unto Me, Jesus whispers . . .
O' the sweetest phrase, I've ever heard.

Come unto Me, my little one . . .
such compassion, hope and love
Come unto Me, Jesus tells me . . .
sweet syllables falling from above.

Come unto Me, my child,
and I will give you rest . . .
Come unto Me, Jesus calls
O' how my soul, these words bless!

https://poetrybydeborahann.wordpress.com/

Week One Discussion Questions

1. What is keeping you from moving closer to God?

2. Do you feel like you need to "earn" your spot at the feet of Jesus? If so, why do you think you feel this way?

3. Can you connect more with Mary or with Martha in this week's scripture? Why?

4. What "falsehoods" do we learn about love that keeps us distanced from God?

Bible Stories
From the Heart

Scripture: _____
_____
_____
_____
_____

Observation: _____
_____
_____
_____
_____

Application: _____
_____
_____
_____
_____

Prayer: _____
_____
_____
_____
_____

Week One Art Tutorial

The color version of this illustration is on the back page of this workbook so feel free to check that for reference. I am going to be honest, I struggled illustrating this verse. I tried drawing Jesus and Mary, but just couldn't fit them in the space the way I wanted.

In the end I decided to draw spirals with some hidden meanings. The orange one is Jesus. The large blue one is Mary, and the others are us when we draw close to Him. And then I added details of dots to add to the overall drawing. Here's how you can do the same:

1. Start with the biggest spiral on the left side of the paper. It is a lot like a super scrolly question mark.

2. Draw the circles at the bend of the spiral. And under that start the blue scroll.

3. From there add more scrolls that fill the bottom of the page. Add little circles.

4. Write in the Bible verse, using capital letters to emphasize key words.

5. Add color.

...but ONE thing is NEEDED. & Mary has chosen that GOOD PART, that will not be taken from her. Luke 10:42

Nicole Plymesser Nelson 2016

Week Two Lesson

Week Two Introduction

Does God truly want to be near someone like ME?

For many of us, this is a concern that stops us from drawing closer to our Father.

The remarkable fact is that He truly does desire for each one of us to come to Him. Through these lessons we will discover that Christ sincerely longs for us to draw closer to Him each and every day.

Let's look closely at both Jesus' words and actions to help us to see this.

Focus Scripture

While on earth- Jesus welcomed everyone to draw closer to Him and to the LOVE of God (He especially welcomed sinners!)

Mark 2:13-17 (NKJV)
13 Then He went out again by the sea; and all the multitude came to Him, and He taught them. 14 As He passed by, He saw Levi the son of Alphaeus sitting at the tax office. And He said to him, "Follow Me." So he arose and followed Him.

15 Now it happened, as He was dining in Levi's house, that many tax collectors and sinners also sat together with Jesus and His disciples; for there were many, and they followed Him. 16 And when the scribes and Pharisees saw Him eating with the tax collectors and sinners, they said to His disciples, "How is it that He eats and drinks with tax collectors and sinners?"

17 When Jesus heard it, He said to them, "Those who are well have no need of a physician, but those who are sick. I did not come to call the righteous, but sinners, to repentance."

Biblical History

Matthew (Levi) in the Bible came to be one of Jesus' disciples. Before Matthew became a disciple of Christ, he was a tax collector. Matthew aka Levi (in the above verses) are the same person.

Tax collectors, like Levi, were hated by the Jews because they worked for the Roman government. The Roman government at this time in history was an enemy of the Jewish people.

Even though the Roman government was against both the Jewish faith and lifestyle, some Jewish men chose to work for them as tax collectors. These Jewish men did this as a way to get wealthy. These tax collectors not only worked for the "enemy", but they were oftentimes very dishonest individuals.

These men would very often demand more "tax" money than what was owed in an attempt to cheat their neighbors. Because of these reasons, tax collectors were known to their Jewish neighbors as horrible people and terrible sinners.

Since Matthew (Levi) was a tax collector, he was looked upon this way by his community. Religious people stayed clear of people like Matthew. A "good" Jewish person would have never been seen dining with a tax collector.

These negative opinions and dirty details did not concern Jesus. Our loving Savior was not worried about what the so-called religious people thought. He loved Matthew (Levi) even in his sinful state.

The fact that Jesus invited Levi (a sinful tax collector) to draw nearer to Him is so amazing. God loved Levi. He loves each one of us with that same mighty passion. Even though we sin and fall short on a daily basis, God truly does want each of us to come closer!

Thoughts from Leslie

Our sins do not keep God from longing to be near to us.

This is so beautiful to me! :) Our human minds cannot comprehend the powerful emotion that God feels towards us. He deeply desires for each one of us to draw nearer to Him. He truly does long to be close to us each and every day! This is so incredible!

Think about the strongest feelings of Love that you have ever experienced. The feelings we have felt are only a dim shadow to the amount of love that God feels for us on an ongoing basis. Remember that God IS love!

Focus Words

MONDAY

Mark 2:13-17 (NKJV)
*13 Then He went out again by the sea; and all the multitude came to Him, and He taught them. 14 As He passed by, He saw Levi the son of Alphaeus sitting at the tax office. And He said to him, "**Follow** Me." So he arose and followed Him.*

15 Now it happened, as He was dining in Levi's house, that many tax collectors and sinners also sat together with Jesus and His disciples; for there were many, and they followed Him. 16 And when the scribes and Pharisees saw Him eating with the tax collectors and sinners, they said to His disciples, "How is it that He eats and drinks with tax collectors and sinners?"

17 When Jesus heard it, He said to them, "Those who are well have no need of a physician, but those who are sick. I did not come to call the righteous, but sinners, to repentance."

Follow: (verb)
to walk or proceed along <follow a path or person>

Original word: ἀκολουθέω (akoloutheō)

Definition: properly, to be in the same way with, i.e. to accompany (specially, as a disciple)

Connection to Us

We need to be so careful of who or what we are "following". When we allow another person to lead us, we are in essence accepting their desires as our own. It is human nature for a person to seek their own personal desires. Knowing this should help us to see just how dangerous the act of "following" can be.

Before we decide to follow someone we need to have a clear understanding of just WHERE they are going! I wonder if any of us truly take the time to consider the deep impact that following the wrong person can have on our lives? This can change our entire destiny! As children of God, we KNOW where Jesus is headed. He is always moving toward His Father!

We also know what He desires, He desires for each of us to follow Him as He leads us nearer to His Father, God. He is continuously traveling and continuously leading us in the direction where true LOVE is found!

He is calling us to FOLLOW Him! This is so beautiful! Are we ready to truly say yes to our Savior?

Connection to Me

_____

_____

_____

_____

_____

_____

TUESDAY

Mark 2:13-14 (NKJV)

*13 Then He went out again by the sea; and all the multitude came to Him, and He taught them. 14 As He passed by, He saw Levi the son of Alphaeus sitting at the tax office. And He said to him, "Follow Me." So he **arose** and followed Him.*

Arose: (verb)
to get up

Original Word: ἀνίστημι (anistēmi)

Definition: to stand up (literal or figurative)

Connection to Us

Jesus wants us to be an active participant in our faith walk with Him. Growing nearer to our Lord is something that we must actively pursue to achieve. It is by no means something that happens by chance. In order to pursue it, we must be willing to STAND UP, be an active participant, and actually MOVE. Before we can follow our Lord and Savior where He desires to lead us, we must ARISE!

Connect this theory with the app, "Couch to 5K". This running app helps nonrunners train and exercise in a slow and steady way. Notice it is titled COUCH to 5k. The first step to accomplishing the ultimate 5K goal is to first ARISE off of the couch!

It is the same in ANY area of your life in which you are wanting to GROW. You must first ARISE!

Are you ready to ARISE?

Connection to Me

_____

_____

_____

_____

_____

_____

Mark 2:13-17 (NKJV)

13 Then He went out again by the sea; and all the multitude came to Him, and He taught them. 14 As He passed by, He saw Levi the son of Alphaeus sitting at the tax office. And He said to him, "Follow Me." So he arose and followed Him.

*15 Now it happened, as He was **dining** in Levi's house, that many tax collectors and sinners also sat together with Jesus and His disciples; for there were many, and they followed Him. 16 And when the scribes and Pharisees saw Him eating with the tax collectors and sinners, they said to His disciples, "How is it that He eats and drinks with tax collectors and sinners?"*

17 When Jesus heard it, He said to them, "Those who are well have no need of a physician, but those who are sick. I did not come to call the righteous, but sinners, to repentance."

Dining: (verb)
to eat a meal.

Original Word: κατάκειμαιτο (katakeimai)

Definition: to recline at a meal

Connection to Us

When we look at the definition for the word dine, it is easy to miss the significance of this simple act. The fact that Jesus dined with sinners is extremely important!

When people dined together in Biblical times, it was a very meaningful event. It was a way of showing both love and acceptance. When Jesus chose to dine with this group of people "in essence" he was announcing to everyone in that town that He LOVED and accepted these people. He was not saying that He agreed with their lifestyles, but He is saying that He LOVED them in spite of their lifestyles!

Think back to when you were in high school. Who we sat with at lunch was very important. Our "table mates" had a HUGE effect on how the rest of the school population viewed us. Who we sat with would immediately put us into a certain category: we were immediately labeled as a jock, a nerd, a popular kid, etc.

This was kind of the same silly thinking back in Jesus' day. In the eyes of those around him, Jesus, by choosing to dine with "sinners" was put in a VERY QUESTIONABLE category.

Because He was choosing to dine with sinners… did this make HIM a sinner?

This was the question that was running through some "religious" people's minds. Jesus did not worry Himself as to what people thought about Him. He LOVED these "sinful" people and He DEEPLY desired to spend time with them. He feels the same towards each one of us today! This is true LOVE! This is so incredible!

Are we ready to invite Jesus to spend time with us today?

He is eagerly waiting to "dine" with us!

Connection to Me

_____

_____

_____

_____

_____

_____

<u>THURSDAY</u>

Mark 2:13-17 (NKJV)
13 Then He went out again by the sea; and all the multitude came to Him, and He taught them. 14 As He passed by, He saw Levi the son of Alphaeus sitting at the tax office. And He said to him, "Follow Me." So he arose and followed Him.

15 Now it happened, as He was dining in Levi's house, that many tax collectors and sinners also sat together with Jesus and His disciples; for there were many, and they followed Him. 16 And when the scribes and Pharisees saw Him eating with the tax collectors and sinners, they said to His disciples, "How is it that He eats and drinks with tax collectors and sinners?"

*17 When Jesus heard it, He said to them, "Those who are well have no need of a physician, but those who are sick. I did not come to **call** the righteous, but sinners, to repentance."*

Call: (verb)
to command or request to come or be present

Original Word: λέγω (legō)

Definition: (a) I call, summon, invite, (b) I call, name.

Connection to Us

Jesus does not command any of us to come to Him, but He does CALL for us to come closer. Jesus is "the way, the truth, and the light." He could simply stand at a distance watching us and thinking to Himself, "Those silly children. They should KNOW I will lead them to my Father. They should KNOW I will lead them on the path toward true love! If they choose NOT to follow me, that is their own sad loss! It is no 'skin off my back.' I am just going to stand here and watch them wander in darkness."

But Our Savior DOESN'T say that! Our Messiah actually DID give the skin off of His back the day that He chose to die on the cross for our sins! And now He does not passively sit by and look down on us whenever we roam around in darkness - He continues to CALL TO US to follow Him. He is lovingly leading us toward the LIGHT!!! It is up to us to FOLLOW! This is so beautiful! Are we ready to answer His CALL today?

Connection to Me

_____

_____

_____

_____

_____

_____

_____

Strategy for This Week: Drawing Nearer

Intentionally sit and reflect upon today's lesson.

Ask God to help you release all of your problems to Him - even the ones you are not aware of at this time.

As you relax your mind and body, start coloring this week's coloring page as you intentionally seek God's presence. He is right there beside you!

Take the time to talk to your Heavenly Father. Ask Him to reveal Himself to you.

Thank Him for loving you in such a deep and meaningful way!

Sinners Wanted!
By Deborah Ann Belka

A job posting that is always open . . .

Sinners wanted,
inquire within . . .
looking for those
willing to die to sin.

Experience needed,
in both greed and pride looking for those
eager to be My bride.

Seeking those skillful,
in lying, murder, and stealing
looking for those
who need a spiritual healing.

Knowledge appreciated,
in selfishness and conceit
looking for those
who need a Savior to meet.

Practice in immorality,
Isn't the only must
Looking for those
Who want to conquer every lust.

If you are interested,
come right on in . . .
I have been wondering
where you have been!

Week Two Discussion Questions

1. Jesus saw Levi sitting in his tax collection office and called for him to come to Him. Levi was a "sinner" and Jesus still wanted to be close to him. How does this fact help you understand the love of God?

2. Levi was so excited about Jesus coming to His house that he invited all of his friends to come to dinner too. Have you invited your friends to spend time with you and Jesus lately? If not, what do you feel is stopping you?

3. Instead of Jesus entering the tax office and eating with Levi there, He directed him to "follow him." This required Levi to leave the tax office. What do you think is the relevance of this?

Bible Stories
From the Heart

Scripture: _____

_____

_____

_____

_____

_____

Observation: _____

_____

_____

_____

_____

_____

Application: _____

_____

_____

_____

_____

_____

Prayer: _____

_____

_____

_____

_____

_____

Week Two Art Tutorial

Nicole Plymesser Nelson 2016

Jesus is calling to us here and I kept it simple: Just a talk bubble with Jesus' words and the sun/the light of the world to represent His presence.

1. Start by drawing the talk bubble shape...just a big lumpy circle, but instead of closing it you bring it down to create the tail.

2. I used the two edges of the tail to then draw a frame around the piece to contain the sky.

3. Add a few shapes of clouds in the background.

4. Draw the sun in the corner, starting with a circle, then the points, and last the spirals on the tips.

5. Add the words of the verse in the talk bubble.

6. And color.

Nicole Plymesser Nelson 2016

Week Three Lesson

Week Three Introduction

Moving closer to our Lord can sometimes be overwhelming.

Satan will often fill us with silly thoughts such as:

Does God even care about me?

Can I really trust Him to provide and protect me?

The answer to both is YES!

God loves and cares for us more than we can ever imagine! God has always been with His children. He has both protected and loved them since the beginning of time. He continues to do the same for each of us today.

In our focus verses for this week, the author reminds God's children about some of the mighty things the Lord has done in the past to protect and care for His people.

The early Israelites had witnessed God's amazing power first-hand each time God stepped in to deliver them from enemy forces. We can read about these first-hand accounts in the book of Exodus.

Moses documented these divine accounts. Because of this, we are able know all about God's incredible power and protection for His children from the very beginning of time.

Even though we no longer have the need to escape enemy chariots, we still need God's power and protection on a daily basis. We live in a spiritual world. We are in danger of experiencing Satan's attacks on any given day.   The difference is, that unlike the Israelites' past attacks from enemy armies and war chariots, many times we are unaware that powerful and dangerous attacks are still coming our way today!

But God is aware! He is always ready and willing to provide us needed protection. It is so wonderful to realize that our God never changes! He cared for His people in the past and He STILL cares for His people today!

He truly desires to take care of us!

And He deeply longs for us to draw NEAR to Him.

Throughout this week, we will spend time remembering and reflecting upon everything we know about our Heavenly Father's provisions and protection.

We will do this both by reflecting upon Biblical examples and by recalling examples from our own lives.

Let's get started!

Focus Verse

Psalm 46: 7-11 (NKJV)
7 The Lord of hosts is with us; The God of Jacob is our refuge. Selah 8 Come, behold the works of the Lord, Who has made desolations in the earth. 9 He makes wars cease to the end of the earth; He breaks the bow and cuts the spear in two; He burns the chariot in the fire. 10 Be still, and know that I am God; I will be exalted among the nations, I will be exalted in the earth! 11 The Lord of hosts is with us; The God of Jacob is our refuge. Selah

Biblical History

We do not know for sure who wrote this psalm, but we do know that is was meant to be sang by God's children as a song of remembrance. Whoever wrote this song (psalm) did so with the intention of bringing the Israelites peace during times of uncertainty. Likewise, this psalm along with examples below, can be used to continue to bring each of us peace today.

There are several examples in the Bible of God specifically protecting and providing for His people. The Israelites were often reminded of these times through the psalms they would sing.

Here are just a few examples: God protected the Israelites from the Egyptians (14:13-31), he provided manna for them (16:4-5) and he gave them victory over the Amalekites (17:8-16).

It is important to note that in verse 11 when the author states that the Lord of hosts is with us, the "*us*" is referring to literally *us* – all of God's children This includes you and me!

Thoughts from Leslie

Our minds can sometimes play tricks on us. Sadly, even when we know something is true, our thoughts can sometimes deceive us. Because of this, it is vital for each of us to use our eyes and minds to SEEK the truth!

As most of us know, seeing the truth is sometimes easier said than done. What makes seeing the truth most difficult is that we are often given a very limited view of a situation. This is very true when it comes to seeing the truth about God.

Because our views are limited, Satan will continuously try to feed us lies. Satan will work to make us believe that God is not there for us. The devil will tell us that we are wasting our time by trying to draw nearer to our Heavenly Father. We must remember that Satan is a liar!

It is up to us to both SEEK and SEE the truth! We can do this by intentionally looking for God in our life. Doing this will help us to see through the lies of Satan. Each time we see God's love and protection for us, let's challenge ourselves to actually acknowledge and document it!

Humans are known to have short term memories. That is why it is imperative for us to actually recall and reflect upon God's incredible goodness on a daily basis.

Because it is sometimes hard for us to remember all of the details regarding God's LOVE for us, it is important for us to take some needed time to stimulate our brains. Music can help with this! After we finish this lesson, let's listen to some inspiring songs and reflect upon all of the ways that God has cared for us in the past.

Why the need to add music to our times with Jesus? Scientific studies have shown that people respond very strongly to music. Some studies have shown that music can stimulate more parts of the brain than any other human activity.

Music can have a very positive effect on our thoughts (if we choose the right music). Early humans understood this. I think that is why the book of Psalms is so very powerful! Let's learn from the author of this psalm.

Let's first behold the works of God (by remembering and listing all the ways the Lord has cared for us in the past). Next, let's be still and KNOW that He is God (by relaxing in His presence as we color and soak in His Love for us). Are we ready?

Focus Words

MONDAY

Psalm 46: 7-11 (NKJV)
*7 The **Lord of hosts** is with us; The God of Jacob is our refuge. Selah 8 Come, behold the works of the Lord, Who has made desolations in the earth. 9 He makes wars cease to the end of the earth; He breaks the bow and cuts the spear in two; He burns the chariot in the fire. 10 Be still, and know that I am God; I will be exalted among the nations, I will be exalted in the earth! 11 The Lord of hosts is with us; The God of Jacob is our refuge. Selah*

Lord of hosts – hosts: (noun); <u>army</u> : a great number: <u>multitude</u>

Original word: צבאה צבא-tsāḇāʾ tsebāʾāh (tsaw-baw', tseb-aw-aw')

Definition: that which goes forth, army, war, warfare, host (of organized army), host (of angels)

Connection to Us

Most countries required their citizens to pay taxes. In exchange for a percentage of these taxes, military protection is provided for the citizens. The purpose of this military protection is to keep the counties and its individuals safe in case there is ever a physical attack made by an enemy. This is a good thing because our physical protection is very important!

What is often overlooked is our need for spiritual protection. We sometimes forget that we live in a spiritual world. Because we live in a spiritual word, we need spiritual protection just as much as physical protection.

Satan and his crew are relentlessly plotting and scheming in the hopes of personally destroying us. Their goal is to attack us when we are unprotected and at our weakest. Luckily for us, we don't have be unprotected!

If we are a child of God, we have our Heavenly Father and His host of angels ready to fight for us! That is the reminder given in this week's scripture. Let's read this verse again and actually visualize a host (a great number) of angels surrounding us.

This is a POWERFUL image! God loves us so incredibly much! He deeply desires us to Draw in NEARER to Him. He longs for us to rest under his powerful arms of protection!

Connection to Me

_____

_____

_____

_____

_____

_____

TUESDAY

Psalm 46: 7-11 (NKJV)
7 The Lord of hosts is with us; The God of Jacob is our **refuge**. Selah 8 Come, behold the works of the Lord, Who has made desolations in the earth. 9 He makes wars cease to the end of the earth; He breaks the bow and cuts the spear in two; He burns the chariot in the fire. 10 Be still, and know that I am God; I will be exalted among the nations, I will be exalted in the earth! 11 The Lord of hosts is with us; The God of Jacob is our refuge. Selah

Refuge: (noun)
shelter or protection from danger or distress, a place that provides shelter or protection

Original Word: משׂגּב (mis gab mis-gawb')

Definition: high place, refuge, secure height, retreat, stronghold

Connection to Us

How many of us remember being scared as a child? The first place we would run is to the loving embrace of our parent. We would lift our arms up to our mom or dad in the hopes that they would pick us up and carry us away from the "perceived" danger. As Christians, we can still have that parental protection.

Our Heavenly Father is offering His loving embrace to each one of us today! We are HIS children! He is calling for us to reach our arms to Him! He longs to HOLD and CARRY us away from the "real" and "ever present" danger that our current world holds. Satan is grabbing at us! Real Danger is HERE! Are we ready to jump into the protective arms of our Almighty Father?

Connection to Me

_____

_____

_____

_____

_____

_____

WEDNESDAY

Psalm 46: 7-11 (NKJV)
7 The Lord of hosts is with us; The God of Jacob is our refuge. Selah 8 Come, **behold** the works of the Lord, Who has made desolations in the earth. 9 He makes wars cease to the end of the earth; He breaks the bow and cuts the spear in two; He burns the chariot in the fire. 10 Be still, and know that I am God; I will be exalted among the nations, I will be exalted in the earth! 11 The Lord of hosts is with us; The God of Jacob is our refuge. Selah

Behold: (verb)
to look at (something): to see (something)

Original Word: חָזָה (châzâh khaw-zaw)

Definition: to gaze at; mentally to perceive, contemplate (with pleasure), specifically to have a vision of

Connection to Us

Most of us have had issues in our lives which have caused us to feel uneasy and even a little nervous. Those issues may have involved something worrisome such as a health scare, a financial burden, a family crisis, a romantic conflict, etc. Whatever the issues were or are we have a choice to make.

The choice involves which we will choose to empower. Are we going to empower our issue or are we going to empower our God?

At what (or WHO) are we going to "behold"? If we choose to LOOK continuously at our problem, our problem will seem to GROW! In the same way, if we intentionally LOOK at our Lord, our FAITH in our Heavenly Father will GROW!
It is up to us which we "feed"!

We can choose to empower the issue we are having, or we can choose to empower our faith!

Are we ready to turn our eyes away from our issue for a moment and BEHOLD God's amazing power to protect and provide?

Let's spend some time today FEEDING our faith. To do this, let's go back and reflect upon all of the ways that God protected and provided for His children in the past. Our God NEVER changes! He has and will always take care of His flock! Let's review again the "Biblical History" section for this week's devotion to be reminded of the short list of God's protection shown in the past.

God protected the Israelites from the Egyptians (Exodus 14:13-31), he provided manna for them (Exodus 16:4-5) and he gave them victory over the Amalekites (Exodus 17:8-16). I challenge you to research some other Biblical examples and add them to that list this week. The book of Exodus is a GREAT place to look :)

Connection to Me

_____

_____

_____

_____

_____

_____

THURSDAY

Psalm 46: 7-11 (NKJV)
*7 The Lord of hosts is with us; The God of Jacob is our refuge. Selah 8 Come, behold the **works** of the Lord, Who has made desolations in the earth. 9 He makes wars cease to the end of the earth; He breaks the bow and cuts the spear in two; He burns the chariot in the fire. 10 Be still, and know that I am God; I will be exalted among the nations, I will be exalted in the earth! 11 The Lord of hosts is with us; The God of Jacob is our refuge. Selah*

Works: (noun)
things that results from the use or fashioning of a particular material

Original Word: מפעל מפעלה (miph'al miph'alah; mif-awl', mif-aw-law')

Definition: works, things made

Connection to Us

As humans we are limited to what we can make or accomplish because our materials are limited. Even talented artists are somewhat limited to the art they can create because of the numbered resources available to them.

It is vital for us to understand that God does not have limited resources or materials! Our Heavenly Father is WILLING and ABLE to create any WORK that we can ever hope for or imagine!

I think sometimes we limit God with our restricted view of Him. Very often we ask for assistance and even act upon a choice that is so much lower than the choice that God is wanting to WORK for us. We do this just because we do not fully understand and trust in His abilities!

We must remember that Our Heavenly Father created EVERYTHING! He is not limited by resources, materials, time, or man power! This fact is so much deeper than our earthly minds can even understand!

Let's ask God today to help us grow in our understanding and faith in His abilities and potential WORKS! Let's pray that our desires and "asks" do not limit God in any way. Many times our minds do not even know WHAT to ask for; this is why it is imperative that we pray for God to do HIS will in our lives! The biggest challenge after we pray is to wait. Many times we are tempted to "HELP" God. When we do this we are actually just getting in the way of His PERFECT PLAN for us!

Let's pray for FAITH and PATIENCE as we ask for and allow God to WORK in each one of our lives in HIS WAY this coming week :)

Connection to Me

_____

_____

_____

_____

_____

_____

Strategy for This Week: Drawing Nearer

For the first few minutes, let's simply listen to our favorite worship songs and direct our thoughts to God.

As our brains begin to remember examples of God's LOVE in our lives, let's actually write these examples down. This list will be important for us to keep nearby. These examples can be a constant reminder to us of who God is!

After you finish your list, sit quietly and color for the remainder of the time.

Let's thank God for loving us and ask Him to reveal Himself in a new and powerful way to each one of us today!

In God Alone
By Deborah Ann Belka

In God and Him alone,
my soul waits ever patiently
for my hope only comes
when I rest sound and quietly.

He is my sturdy Rock,
from which I can't be shaken
He protects and defends me
from the attacks of Satan.

A Refuge to me He is,
a place to run and hide
His love encompasses me
from each and every side.

It is in Him I trust,
in Him my faith is hedged
for He is my soul's salvation
in His strength I am dredged.

In God and Him alone,
my soul rests expectantly
nothing can move me from
waiting on Him patiently!

Week Three Discussion Questions

1. Have you ever been tricked into believing a lie? How did it happen?

2. Satan does not want us to trust God with our problems. He wants each one of us to try to solve issues using our own power. Why do you think this is?

3. Has Satan tricked you recently into believing that there is a problem in your life that you should not release to God? What exactly is this problem?

4. Beginning today, what can you do differently to help yourself not believe Satan's lies?

5. Do you feel like you place limits on God? If so, how can you work to break this habit?

Bible Stories
From the Heart

Scripture:_____

_____

_____

_____

_____

_____

Observation:_____

_____

_____

_____

_____

_____

Application:_____

_____

_____

_____

_____

_____

Prayer:_____

_____

_____

_____

_____

_____

Week Three Art Tutorial

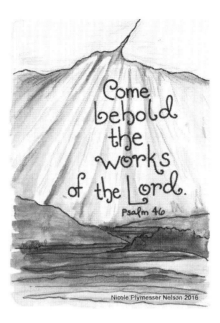

Nothing is more impressive to me than nature--God is so creative and amazing! Whenever I see rays of light coming through clouds I think of God shining down on us. I even like to think of angels sliding down them coming to each of us.

1. Start 2/3 of the way down the paper. Draw one very lumpy line to create the horizon.
2. Form the islands/land jutting into the water by making a straight line that goes back to the right for the land on the right side of the paper. On the left extend the lumpy line down a little and then pull it back to the right to form that land. Then draw an extra bumpy half circle under those to be the third land mass.
3. Add horizontal lines to be the top/currents of water.
4. In the center of the paper write the Bible verse. Start with simple printed letters and add in the extra curl.
5. Above that draw in the two cloud shapes so there will be one spot where the sun can come through.
6. When you add color, add in the rays of sunshine coming from the break in the clouds.

Come behold the works of the Lord.

Psalm 46

Nicole Plymesser Nelson 2016

Week Four Lesson

Week Four Introduction

The purpose of this study is to move us closer to the love of our Heavenly Father.

Once we move closer, our goal is to remain there.

Spending quiet time reflecting and meditating on God's goodness can help us to achieve this goal.

Are you ready to relax and remain at the feel of Jesus?

If so, this lesson is for you!

Focus Verses

Philippians 4:6-8 (NKJV)
6 Be anxious for nothing, but in everything by prayer and supplication, with thanksgiving, let your requests be made known to God; 7 and the peace of God, which surpasses all understanding, will guard your hearts and minds through Christ Jesus. 8 Finally, brethren, **whatever things are true, whatever things are noble, whatever things are just, whatever things are pure, whatever things are lovely, whatever things are of good report, if there is any virtue and if there is anything praiseworthy–meditate on these things.**

Biblical History

The book of Philippians was written by Paul. He was one of the greatest Christian missionaries of all times. At this time in history it was very dangerous for a person to spread their beliefs regarding Jesus.

During these early years of the church there were several groups of powerful people who wanted to end the spread of Christianity. Because these people desired to destroy the early church, it was not uncommon for early Christian leaders to be both tortured and even imprisoned for their faith. Paul was one of these targeted leaders. He had been beaten and imprisoned more than once for his missionary work. Throughout all of this turbulence and hardship, Paul never lost faith in God. When chapter four of Philippians was written, Paul was actually being held in a prison cell.

What kept Paul strong throughout his many prison stays was reflecting and meditating on God's great LOVE and protection for him in the past.

In this chapter, Paul was writing to a group of church members in Philippi.   He was in prison, yet Paul was writing to encourage his fellow brothers and sisters in Christ. He was encouraging them to not be anxious. This is incredible! Paul had every reason to be both anxious and worried, yet he chose to be the opposite. He chose to meditate on the positive and look to God's prior love and provisions to uphold him! In doing this he was able to remain steadfast in both his joy and faith.

We can learn a powerful lesson from Paul! Through Paul we will be reminded that **our focus controls our outlook!** :)

As we continue to discover the deep and loving nature of God, we will not only be growing in our faith, we will also be getting more and more comfortable sitting at His feet. It is human nature that people usually feel a little bit uneasy sitting really close to people who are unfamiliar to them. Think about the last time you went to the movies or even sat on a church pew. Unless you knew the people you are about to sit by, you probably chose to sit away from them.

Before we sit at the feet of someone, we must first really KNOW them. We must not only KNOW them, but we must also have a sense that this person actually cares for us. Why else would we choose to sit within "kicking" distance of someone's foot?

As we sit at the feet of Jesus, He wants us to know that He truly does care about us! He sincerely desires to be fully KNOWN by us! The Lord wants us to feel absolutely comfortable and totally willing to draw near to Him!

We learned through a previous devotion that in order to honestly know and trust who God is, we should behold and reflect upon the Lord's past provisions in each one of our lives.

For this reason, this week we will be writing lists of all of the ways that God has proven His love to us. We will write down all of the ways that God had shown us that He loves and cares for us. To help us learn how to meditate, let's keep these lists near to us throughout this week and look at them often.

Before you go any farther, grab a pencil and paper and begin your list now.

Focus Words

MONDAY

Philippians 4:6-8 (NKJV)
*6 Be **anxious** for **nothing**, but in everything by prayer and supplication, with thanksgiving, let your requests be made known to God; 7 and the peace of God, which surpasses all understanding, will guard your hearts and minds through Christ Jesus. 8 Finally, brethren, whatever things are true, whatever things are noble, whatever things are just, whatever things are pure, whatever things are lovely, whatever things are of good report, if there is any virtue and if there is anything praiseworthy–meditate on these things.*

Anxious: (adjective)
drawn in opposite directions; "divided into parts"

Original Word: μεριμνάω (merimnaō, mer-im-nah'-o)

Definition: I am anxious, distracted

Nothing: (pronoun)
no single thing, not a thing

Original Word: μηδείς (mēden; may-den')

Definition: not even one (man, woman, thing)

Usage: any (man, thing), no (man), none, not (at all, any man, a whit), nothing.

Connection to Us

It is so easy to make exceptions to rules *especially when those rules involve us and our emotions.* This verse is literally telling us to not be anxious about ANYTHING! There are no exceptions to that. Be anxious for nothing means exactly that - NOTHING!

God is completely aware of every issue that we are dealing with at any given time. **There are absolutely NO issues which would be an exception to this verse.**

God wants us to hand over ALL of our worries to Him. He does not want our minds filled with anxiety over ANY problem or issue – no matter how big or small. This is sometimes difficult for us, but we can do it!

Let's ask our Heavenly Father to help us!

Connection to Me

_____

_____

_____

_____

_____

_____

Challenge Activity for Today

1. Write down every worry or concern that you can think of.
2. Color code each statement.
3. Choose one color to underline (code) what you consider to be the "big" worries and another color to underline (code) the "small" worries.
4. After you have "coded" each issue, choose a third color.

5. With the third color completely cross out each statement.
6. Finally, using this same third color- write "GOD WILL HANDLE THIS" beside each statement.

Pray again and THANK God for His continuous protection and provision in your life.

TUESDAY

Philippians 4:6-8 (NKJV)
*6 Be anxious for nothing, but in everything by prayer and supplication, with **thanksgiving**, let your requests be made known to God; 7 and the peace of God, which surpasses all understanding, will guard your hearts and minds through Christ Jesus. 8 Finally, brethren, whatever things are true, whatever things are noble, whatever things are just, whatever things are pure, whatever things are lovely, whatever things are of good report, if there is any virtue and if there is anything praiseworthy–meditate on these things.*

thankfulness: (noun)
conscious of benefit received- or *for what we are about to receive.*

Original word: εὐχαριστία (eucharistia; yoo-khar-is-tee'-ah)

Definition: gratitude; actively, grateful language (to God, as an act of worship)

Connection to Us

Notice in the definition of thankfulness it mentions "a consciousness" of what we are **about to receive** - this is HUGE!

This means that as soon as we ask God to resolve an issue - it is resolved! God immediately works out the perfect solution! Because of this, we need to go ahead and THANK Him and move forward actually knowing that God has once again provided!

It is vital for us to understand that He as soon as we ask, God creates the perfect solution tailored specifically for us. Once this solution has been created by God, we must be LED to it! This is where faith and patience come in.

It is at this point that we must relax and allow our Heavenly Father to guide us! If we remain steadfast and follow Him, God will LEAD us to the solution. We must not get anxious and actually snatch our problem back. This is critical!

If we want to achieve the perfect ending that God has designed for us, we must remain on His path!

Connection to Me

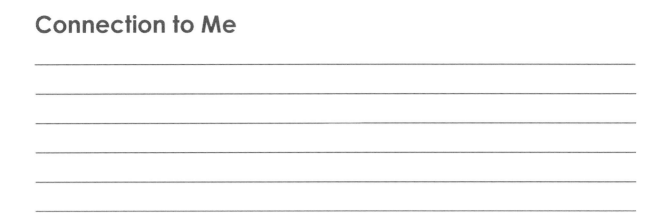

<u>**WEDNESDAY**</u>

Philippians 4:6-8 (NKJV)
6 Be anxious for nothing, but in everything by prayer and supplication, with thanksgiving, let your requests be made known to God; 7 and the **peace** *of God, which surpasses all understanding, will guard your hearts and minds through Christ Jesus. 8 Finally, brethren, whatever things are true, whatever things are noble, whatever things are just, whatever things are pure, whatever things are lovely, whatever things are of good report, if there is any virtue and if there is anything praiseworthy–meditate on these things.*

Peace: (noun)
a state of tranquility or quiet, freedom from disquieting or oppressive thoughts or emotion, harmony in personal relations.

Original Word: εἰρήνη (eirēnē; i-rah'-nay)

Definition: peace (literally or figuratively); by implication, prosperity

Connection to Us

What is the most peaceful place you can think of? The ocean, a mountain trail, a hammock on a spring day? For most of us there is at least one place which represents peace. This is a place which allows us to temporarily leave both the world and our issues behind. When we are there, our worries simply float away in the beauty and tranquility of the surroundings.

The amazing thing is that as children of God, our Heavenly Father is wanting to give us an even GREATER peace! The peace of God is an even more tranquil feeling than even all of these favorite places combined.

It is up to us to search for God's Heavenly peace, but sadly this "spiritual" feeling is sometimes difficult for us to totally experience.

Because we are physical beings who are loved and cared for by a spiritual God, we need God's help to both connect with Him and feel His peace. When we can't feel Him, we often assume He isn't there. Our minds begin behaving and worrying as if the latter is true, when in reality God's arms are reaching out to us continuously.

Our Heavenly Father desires for us to feel both his embrace and His PEACE each and every day! Starting now let's ask God to help us to FEEL him! Our Heavenly Father is willing and able to help, but we must be sincere in our asking. Are you ready to live life feeling light and free? Let's pray for God to guide us.

Prayer:

Dear Heavenly Father,

You love me so much. You do not want to me to be worried or full of stress. As my Father you are waiting with open arms to calm my mind and give me peace. Please help me to stay in your protective arms and actually feel your PEACE.

I know what peace feels like. I can feel it at certain times when I visit special places. I love the stillness that my mind feels during these times.

I deeply desire to feel an even greater peace, your peace, on a daily basis. I know you also desire for me to feel this. Please help me! I love you so very much. Thank you for loving me with your all powerful love.

In Jesus name I pray,
Amen

Connection to Me

_____

_____

_____

_____

_____

THURSDAY

Philippians 4:6-8 (NKJV)
*6 Be anxious for nothing, but in everything by prayer and supplication, with thanksgiving, let your requests be made known to God; 7 and the peace of God, which surpasses all understanding, will guard your hearts and minds through Christ Jesus. 8 Finally, brethren, whatever things are true, whatever things are noble, whatever things are just, whatever things are pure, whatever things are lovely, whatever things are of good report, if there is any virtue and if there is anything praiseworthy—**meditate** on these things.*

Meditate: (verb)
To dwell on anything in thought; to contemplate; to study; to turn or revolve any subject in the mind.

Original Word: λογίζομαι (logizomai; log-id'-zom-ahee)

Definition: reckon, count, charge with; reason, decide, conclude; think, suppose

Connection to Us

Have you ever noticed how easy it is for our eyes and minds to wander towards our problems? This can be a very dangerous thing! What our minds wander toward often tempts us into action.

It is kind of like driving down the road and getting distracted by signs. For example, we see a sign, our mind begins wandering toward the image we see and then we are tempted to act upon it. One common example is when we see the famous "Hot Now" sign glowing at the local Krispy Kreme!

Although we did not feel hungry before we saw it, when our eyes fell upon the letters, our minds begin to taste that delicious treat. Before we know it, we are then tempted to ACT! We immediately feel like we MUST have a scrumptious doughnut.

Notice how quickly our gaze affected our action. We went from not feeling hungry to feeling starving all within a few seconds! We were tempted to pull through the Krispy Kreme drive thru and cheat on our diet all from a three second glance!
Moral of this story: What we gaze upon can alter our thoughts and actions in very powerful ways!

This can be dangerous with doughnuts but it can really be dangerous when our "gaze" turns towards our problems and off of God.

In these verses, God is not telling us to discount our problems, instead He is reminding us to not be distracted or pulled off course because of them. When we feel anxious over something, even something very small, it becomes very easy for us to make a rash and oftentimes bad decision as a reaction. Our ACTIONS can many times lead to even more anxiety! Our focus verses for this week were written to help us understand this.

When the scripture says to be anxious for nothing, it literally means NOTHING! In these verses, God is reminding us to not focus our gaze on ANYTHING but Him!

It is up to us to direct our gaze, thoughts, and actions! Let's begin by turning our gaze away from worry and back toward peace. Let's intentionally meditate upon God's amazing LOVE!

Connection to Me

_____

_____

_____

_____

_____

_____

Strategy for This Week: Drawing Nearer

For the first few minutes, meditate on your list which you created at the beginning of today's lesson. Take time to personally thank God for each of these examples of His LOVE. Next, ask Him to reveal more past examples of His provisions for you.

Add these new examples to your list.

For the remaining moments, simply enjoy the calming presence of Jesus as you sit as His feet and color.

Listen to your favorite Christian songs.

Allow yourself to feel God's Love and Peace flow inside of you.

Your Heavenly Father LOVES this quiet time with you!

Week Four Discussion Questions

1. Would you describe yourself as an optimist or a pessimist? Why?

2. Do you find it easy or difficult to control your thoughts? Why?

3. If you let your mind run wild, what are you most likely to think about?   Do these thoughts cause worry or peace?

4. How can mediating on the list of God's provisions help you to have a more positive outlook?

Meditate on Me

By Deborah Ann Belka

Meditate on Me,
put aside some time
to spend alone
and ponder Me.

Moan to Me,
groan and whimper
and express
your heart to Me.

Mutter to Me,
sigh and cry
and whisper
your love for Me.

Talk to Me,
hum sweet words
and murmur
your praise to Me.

Pray to Me,
beseech and plea
and implore
your need for Me.

Meditate on Me,
put aside some time
and lose yourself
. . . in Me!

Bible Stories
From the Heart

Scripture: _____

_____

_____

_____

_____

Observation: _____

_____

_____

_____

_____

Application: _____

_____

_____

_____

_____

Prayer: _____

_____

_____

_____

_____

Week Four Art Tutorial

This was a long verse and very wordy! So I focused on the list of important words and put a bullet with them. The curling line represents my thoughts meditating--circling back to what is important and underlining the illustration as a whole. I added flowers, birds, butterflies, a blue sky--things I like to think of to calm me and keep me focused while meditating. You may decide to add little doodles of other things that are special to you.

1. Start with the curling line down the side. Then extend it with straight lines at the top and bottom.

2. Write the words of the verse. For "meditate"--draw simple printed letters but then add the serif (the little line at the tops and bottoms of each letter).

3. Write the list of things to focus on under that. Under each word make a line/rectangle and then add a circle/dot/bullet in front.

4. Add doodles around the page. And add color.

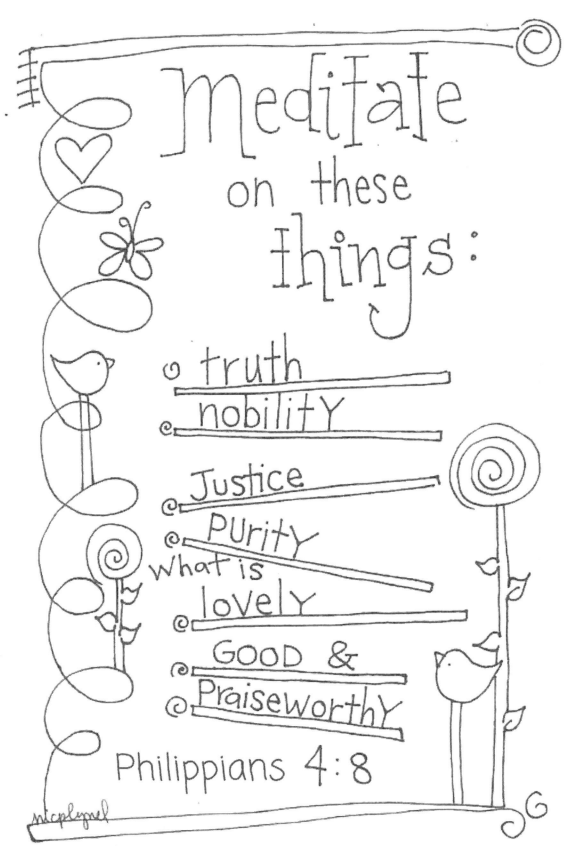

Meditate on these things:

- truth
- nobility
- Justice
- Purity
- What is lovely
- Good & Praiseworthy

Philippians 4:8

Nicole Plymesser Nelson 2016

Week Five Lesson

Week Five Introduction

The purpose of this study is to move us closer to the love of our Heavenly Father. The remarkable fact is that God truly does desire for each one of us to come to Him, but how do we accomplish this? The answer involves humility!

We learned last week that God does not want us to feel anxious about anything no matter how big or small. When we feel anxious we sometimes are tempted to ACT on our own behalf to try to solve our issues.

Many times it is tempting to want to "grab" our problems back from our Heavenly Father, but we must not do this. Because if we do, we are at that point distancing ourselves from God. If our goal is to remain in His presence, we must allow our burdens to REMAIN in His hands!

We must be patient and allow God to SOLVE our problems in His time and in His way. In order to accomplish this, we must be humble!

Focus Verse

1 Peter 5:6-7 (NKJV)
*6 Therefore **humble yourselves under the mighty hand of God**, that He may exalt you in due time, 7 **casting all your care upon Him**, for He cares for you.*

Focus Words

Humble: (verb)
to make low

Original Word: ταπεινόω (tapeinoō; tap-i-no'-o)

Definition: make or bring low, humble

Drawing nearer to our Lord and Savior requires humility. Before we can actually move closer to God we must first be willing to submit our complete control to Him. This includes releasing the grip that we may have on our personal burdens and cares.

These verses are literally saying: before God can exalt us (lift us up out from under our cares/burdens), we must first lower ourselves and bring everything we have under His protective hand. When we humbly relent our cares to God, He can then exalt us from them! Jesus truly does care for us.

Notice the primary first step. We must humble ourselves. This means that we must first stop attempting to "fix" problems on our own. Peter is literally teaching us that before we look to the Lord for help, we must first learn to crawl under God's Almighty Hand.

Biblical History

The author of these verses, Peter, was a former fisherman. Let's learn about the power behind humility through his story. As we read the following verses it is important to note that at this time Peter is known as "Simon"

Luke 5: 1-9 (NKJV)

Simon Peter Is Called

1 So it was, as the multitude pressed about Him to hear the word of God, that He stood by the Lake of Gennesaret, 2 and saw two boats standing by the lake; but the fishermen had gone from them and were washing their nets. 3 Then He got into one of the boats, which was Simon's, and asked him to put out a little from the land. And He sat down and taught the multitudes from the boat.

4 When He had stopped speaking, He said to Simon, "Launch out into the deep and let down your nets for a catch." 5 But Simon answered and said to Him, "Master, we have toiled all night and caught nothing; nevertheless, at Your word I will let down the net." 6 And when they had done this, they caught a great number of fish, and their net was breaking. 7 So they signaled to their partners in the other boat to come and help them. And they came and filled both the boats, so that they began to sink.8 When Simon Peter saw it, he fell down at Jesus' knees, saying, "Depart from me, for I am a sinful man, O Lord!"

9 For he and all who were with him were astonished at the catch of fish which they had taken; 10 and so also were James and John, the sons of Zebedee, who were partners with Simon. And Jesus said to Simon, "Do not be afraid. From now on you will catch men." 11 So when they had brought their boats to land, they forsook all and followed Him.

Let's examine the steps that Simon (Peter) took in order to come to Jesus.

Focus Words

MONDAY

Luke 5: 1-9 (NKJV)

Simon Peter Is Called

1 So it was, as the multitude pressed about Him to hear the word of God, that He stood by the Lake of Gennesaret, 2 and saw two boats standing by the lake; but the fishermen had gone from them and were washing their nets. 3 Then He got into one of the boats, which was Simon's, and asked him to put out a little from the land. And He sat down and taught the multitudes from the boat.

*4 When He had stopped speaking, He said to Simon, "Launch out into the deep and let down your nets for a catch." 5 But Simon answered and said to Him, "Master, we have **toiled** all night and caught nothing; nevertheless, at Your word I will let down the net." 6 And when they had done this, they caught a great number of fish, and their net was breaking. 7 So they signaled to their partners in the other boat to come and help them. And they came and filled both the boats, so that they began to sink.8 When Simon Peter saw it, he fell down at Jesus' knees, saying, "Depart from me, for I am a sinful man, O Lord!"*

9 For he and all who were with him were astonished at the catch of fish which they had taken; 10 and so also were James and John, the sons of Zebedee, who were partners with Simon. And Jesus said to Simon, "Do not be afraid. From now on you will catch men." 11 So when they had brought their boats to land, they forsook all and followed Him.

Toiled: (verb)
work extremely hard or incessantly

Original Word: κοπιάω (kopiaō; kop-ee-ah'-o)

Definition: to feel fatigue; by implication, to work hard

Peter was weighed down under a burden. He had toiled all night, but caught nothing. He depended on catching fish for his livelihood, yet he had worked all day and had not caught a single fish. In a matter of seconds, Peter's outcome was about to change. As we continue to read the story, we see that Jesus Himself was about to exalt this fisherman named Simon. But, before this would happen, Peter had to literally pack up his fishing nets.

Connection to Me

_____

_____

_____

_____

_____

_____

TUESDAY

Luke 5: 1-9 (NKJV)

Simon Peter Is Called

1 So it was, as the multitude pressed about Him to hear the word of God, that He stood by the Lake of Gennesaret, 2 and saw two boats standing by the lake; but the fishermen had gone from them and were washing their nets. 3 Then He got into one of the boats, which was Simon's, and asked him to put out a little from the land. And He sat down and taught the multitudes from the boat.

*4 When He had stopped speaking, He said to Simon, "Launch out into the deep and let down your nets for a catch." 5 But Simon answered and said to Him, "Master, we have toiled all night and caught nothing; nevertheless, at Your word I will **let down** the net."*
6 And when they had done this, they caught a great number of fish, and their net was breaking. 7 So they signaled to their partners in the other boat to come and help them. And they came and filled both the boats, so that they began to sink. 8 When Simon Peter saw it, he fell down at Jesus' knees, saying, "Depart from me, for I am a sinful man, O Lord!"

9 For he and all who were with him were astonished at the catch of fish which they had taken; 10 and so also were James and John, the sons of Zebedee, who were partners with Simon. And Jesus said to Simon, "Do not be afraid. From now on you will catch men."
11 So when they had brought their boats to land, they forsook all and followed Him.

Let down: (verb)
to allow someone or something to move to a lower position

Original word: χαλάω (chalaō; khal-ah'-o)

Definition: let down, lower let down, lower, slacken, loosen.

Peter let down his net a second time, but this time he relied on Jesus to help. (verse 5)

This time Peter depended on God's guidance and mite to help him. It is vital to see that Peter was still responsible to "man" the net, but this time Jesus was there to lead and bless the direction of the "drop".

Jesus does not want us to sit on the sidelines and be simply a spectator in this life. He wants us to be involved in solving our problems, but He wants to guide and direct us first. It is not up to us to figure everything out on our own, we must simply be humble and follow His voice.

Connection to Me

_____

_____

_____

_____

_____

_____

WEDNESDAY

Luke 5: 1-9 (NKJV)

Simon Peter Is Called

1 So it was, as the multitude pressed about Him to hear the word of God, that He stood by the Lake of Gennesaret, 2 and saw two boats standing by the lake; but the fishermen had gone from them and were washing their nets. 3 Then He got into one of the boats, which was Simon's, and asked him to put out a little from the land. And He sat down and taught the multitudes from the boat.

4 When He had stopped speaking, He said to Simon, "Launch out into the deep and let down your nets for a catch." 5 But Simon answered and said to Him, "Master, we have toiled all night and caught nothing; nevertheless, at Your word I will let down the net." 6 And when they had done this, they caught a great number of fish, and their net was breaking. 7 So they signaled to their partners in the other boat to come and help them. And they came and filled both the boats, so that they began to sink.8 When Simon Peter saw it, he fell down at Jesus' knees, saying, "Depart from me, for I am a sinful man, O Lord!"

9 For he and all who were with him were astonished at the catch of fish which they had taken; 10 and so also were James and John, the sons of Zebedee, who were partners with Simon. And Jesus said to Simon, "Do not be afraid. From now on you will catch men." 11 So when they had brought their boats to land, they **forsook** all and followed Him.

forsook: (verb)
renounce or give up

Original Word: ἀφίημιl (aphiēmi; af-ee'-ay-mee)

Definition: send away, release, remit, forgive, permit(a) I send away, (b) I let go, release, permit to depart

Finally, Peter had to release all (including all of his burdens) before he could follow Jesus - verse 11.

Once again, let's look at the symbolism in this verse. Before we can truly draw nearer to Christ we must first lay all our burdens down. Our hands should be light and free so that we can hold onto His mighty right hand.

I love how Simon did not have to catch any fish (solve any of his problem) before he was invited to abide with Jesus.

I also love how Jesus asked Simon to **forsake all**.

Let this be a lesson for us. We can totally depend on Jesus to solve our problems, but we must first release control of our burdens. This means that we must intentionally **lay our burdens down.**

Connection to Me

_____

_____

_____

_____

_____

_____

THURSDAY

1 Peter 5:6-7 (NKJV)
6 Therefore **humble** yourselves under the mighty hand of God, that He may exalt you in due time, 7 casting all your care upon Him, for He cares for you.

Humble: (verb)
to make low

Original Word: ταπεινόω (prospiptō; pros-pip'-to)

Definition: drop close to the ground

Drawing nearer to our Lord and Savior requires humility. Before we can actually move closer to God we must first be willing to submit our complete control to Him. This includes releasing the grip that we may have on our personal burdens and cares.

What do you need to release to your Savior today?

Connection to Us

As women it is hard for us to admit that we cannot fix every problem. After all, mending broken things is our specialty. Women are experts at repairing damaged toys, calming hurt feelings, and retrieving "lost" objects.

If we are incapable to fix a problem, we will wear ourselves out trying to repair it anyway. It is very hard for us to admit defeat. After all, as women we should be able to fix everything that goes wrong in our lives. RIGHT? WRONG!

It is this type of thinking that gets us into trouble. It is this type of thinking that Satan wants women to believe. In our scripture today, Peter is instructing us to humble ourselves. This is usually easier said than done!

Admitting that we cannot resolve troubles on our own is where humility comes in. Acknowledging that we need help from God should never make us feel weak or like less of a woman. Having the power and might of The Creator of the Universe available to us anytime day or night should actually make us feel more like a fierce superwoman than an inadequate failure.

We must never forget that we are living in a spiritual world.

The issues we face cannot always be fixed by adding glue or even by applying a Barbie band aid. There is nothing we can purchase through Amazon or at the mall that will ultimately give us more power! The only way to achieve victory in these battles is by allowing God to do our fighting for us.

For victory's sake - we must humble ourselves and draw nearer to God!

Connection to Me

_____

_____

_____

_____

_____

Strategy for this week: Drawing Nearer

Intentionally sit and reflect upon today's lesson. Ask God to help you release all of your problems to Him - even the ones you are not aware of at this time. As you relax your mind and body, start coloring this week's coloring page. Intentionally seek God's presence. He is right there beside you! Talk to your Heavenly Father. Ask Him to reveal Himself to you. Thank Him for loving you in such a deep and meaningful way!

Prayer

Dear Heavenly Father,

I deeply desire to draw nearer to you. I am so grateful that you want me near to you. Please help me to totally move into your loving presence. It is one thing to believe in You, it is another to willingly MOVE toward You. Please help me each and every day to draw nearer. I know I need to bring my burdens with me.

Please help me to not only pack up my burdens, but to also release them to you. To do this I need you to help me loosen my grip on my burdens, sorrows, and worries. Father, I need you to lead and help me. I desperately need you to teach me how to truly be humble and dependent on you.

Thank you for loving me! Help me to release everything I am and have over to YOU!

In Jesus name I pray,
Amen.

Life's Burdens

By Deborah Ann Belka

When difficulties come at you,
and troubles are all around
when worried about life's burdens
and their hurdles you can't bound.

That's when you need to take a grip,
hold on to God's righteous hand
for, Jesus won't let you fall
and in His strength you will stand.

When problems can't be solved,
and you have nowhere else to turn
when others try to help you out
but your fears they can't discern.

That's when you need to take hold,
of God's mighty right hand
for, Jesus won't let you down
all your anxieties He'll understand.

When life hands you a lemon,
but you don't like lemonade . . .
when all those around you
fail to come to your aid.

That's when you need to give up,
and rest in His loving hands
for, Jesus wants you to grasp
He has for you, His own plans!

Week Five Discussion Questions

1. What is the number one thing in your life that you are trying to "fix" at this moment?

2. What steps have you already taken?

3. What improvements have you seen, if any?

4. Are other areas in your life suffering as a result of your excessive attention to this one issue? If so, name these overlooked areas.

5. What do you think would happen if you laid your "net" down at the feet of Jesus?

6. What is your big takeaway from this lesson?

Bible Stories
From the Heart

Scripture:_____
_____
_____
_____
_____

Observation:_____
_____
_____
_____
_____

Application:_____
_____
_____
_____
_____

Prayer:_____
_____
_____
_____
_____

Week Five Art Tutorial

This piece is a lot trickier to draw, but it is so worth it! The image of Christ reaching out to us under His mighty hand is powerful.

I used a tutorial from learntodraw.com for some tips on how to draw the hand so let's give credit where it is due!

You use stacks of cylinders to draw the hand. It took lots of erasing--so draw VERY LIGHTLY!

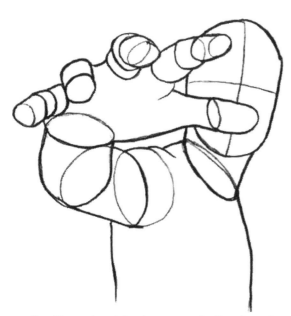

1. Draw the hand first, then draw the arm, then the head. Once you have the elements in place, go ahead and erase and correct any lines that are incorrect in your estimation. Break the drawing up into simple cylinders, so you can see how the various parts fit together. Take it slowly and try and see why the fingers (and arm) appear to look the way they do. If you end up drawing one finger too fat, go ahead and erase and redraw it. Seeing the underlying structure of a figure takes time to master, so keep practicing.

2. After I had the body of Jesus in place, I added lines to be the beard and hair.

3. Then I added a cross in the background so it is obvious who this person is.

4. Finally add the Bible verse under His hand and then add color.

Therefore HUMBLE yourselves under the MIGHTY HAND of GOD that He may EXALT you in due time, casting ALL your /cares upon Him for He CARES for You.
I Peter 5:6-7

Nicole Plymesser Nelson 2016

Bonus Coloring Page

Come
a to
me
all you who
labor
&
are heavy laden
&
I
will give you
Rest.

Matthew 11:28

Nicole Plymesser Nelson 2016

Small Scripture Art for Tracing

THANK YOU!

We hope you learned from this study and grew in your knowledge of God's LOVE for you. Thank you so much for supporting our ministry!

Bible Stories from the Heart creates Adult Coloring Bible Studies that help women read and understand the Bible so they will draw near to God and experience His indescribable love in a new, intimate way.

Our studies feature engaging lessons which include; *Bible History, Word Studies, Reflection Activities, Discussion Questions, Art Projects* and *Coloring Pages*.

If you enjoyed this workbook, we hope you will try some of our other studies.

 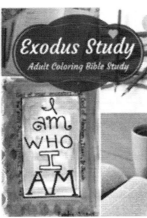  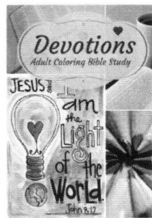

If you haven't already done so, please join our **Bible Stories from the Heart** group on **Facebook**. There, you will join a dynamic, supportive and highly engaged community of thousands of women who participate in our studies and post their artwork to share with other members.

You can find more information on our ministry at: biblestoriesfromtheheart.com.

We would love to hear from you! Please feel to reach us by email with any questions or comments you might have: info@biblestoriesfromtheheart.com.

Thank you!

Made in the USA
San Bernardino, CA
06 January 2019